GET OVER IT!

The Truth About
What You Know
That Just Ain't So!

Paul **H**asselbeck, DDS

Bil **H**olton, Ph.D.

Publisher's Cataloging-in-Publication Data

Hasselbeck, Paul
Get Over It! : The truth about what you know that just ain't so
/ Paul Hasselbeck and Bil Holton
    p. cm.

ISBN 978-1-893095-52-6

Library of Congress Control Number: 2007939553

10 9 8 7 6 5 4 3 2 1

Dedicated to those brave Truth students who are ready to stretch their awareness and move to a whole new level of understanding as they walk the spiritual path on practical feet!

Credits:
Book cover and interior design: Cher Holton

Artwork:
   Unless otherwise indicated: © *2008 www.clipart.com*
   Pg. 163 ~ © Photographer: *May Pang* | Agency: Dreamstime.com

Table of Contents

Introduction

Over the years we have heard and even used some of the phrases that will be debunked in this book. They are familiar euphemisms, platitudes, and stock phrases used by people who come from Unity, New Thought, and New Age backgrounds. Many of these commonly-used expressions have become part of our daily language. Unfortunately, they have also become part of the daily illusion that what we are saying is true.

A few years ago we began to look at these phrases with a more critical eye. We asked ourselves, "Do they reflect the New Thought perspective? Do they say what we actually mean? Or, are they simply traditional theology dressed in new and trendy clothes?"

Journey with us as we explore each of these phrases. We will discover where they are not in alignment with New Thought theology as well as what nuggets of Truth they may contain.

You may feel the urge to defend many of these phrases. They may be ones you have used for many years without questioning their validity. We believe that if you want to dramatically enhance your spiritual walk, you'll consider the wisdom of the old saying attributed to Artemus Ward: "It ain't the things we don't know that hurt us. It's the things we do know that ain't so!"

Think about it. It's not so much the unanswered questions which keep us in the dark; it's the unquestioned answers (traditional, dogmatic beliefs) which keep us stuck in convention. Once upon a time people, intelligent people, believed the world was flat. Of course, we now know that's not true. We've moved beyond that, and many other, archaic assumptions.

We invite you to open your minds and hearts to what we truly believe will be transformational perspectives in the pages which follow. Your current perspectives will be challenged. Your intellectual comfort zones will be thrown off center. The weaknesses of your inherited assumptions will be exposed. But we also believe that the deeper parts of you—your intuitive intelligence, your wise self, your Truth center—will resonate with what we have to say.

For each "Get Over It!" saying, we have included the assumptions behind the phrase that make it so popular, followed by why we believe it is important to "Get Over It!" We then provide what we've entitled a "Truth Triage," which outlines the Truth about the phrase, and why we recommend relanguaging. Finally, we have taken the liberty of providing a "Replacement Phrase," so you can begin to make a consious choice to rephrase what you are saying, in alignment with Truth.

Give yourself a chance to take your consciousness to a higher octave. After reading what we have to say, we hope you will take our perspectives to heart and discover that you have unwittingly used many of these familiar phrases purely out of habit and convention. If that is the conclusion you come to, and we hope it is, we invite you to choose to leave these old, stale expressions behind and remind yourself to "Get Over It" whenever you find yourself using them again.

"It ain't the things we don't know that hurt us. It's the things we do know that ain't so!"
(Artemus Ward, 1834-1867)

So ...
WHAT DO
WE NEED
TO GET
OVER?

What This Phrase Assumes

This phrase is traditional theology dressed in New Thought clothes. The idea of a "cosmic two-by-four" is that there is something or someone outside of us trying to get our attention to teach us an important lesson. The implication is that God, the universe, something "out there" intends to control us for our own good, even if it means harming us or causing us pain. The idea that something wants to get our attention to force us to do what is "right" so it can teach us something is a perspective that abdicates personal choice and responsibility. Further, if we do not "get it" the first time, the whack becomes progressively worse until we finally pay attention.

GET OVER IT!

● ● ● ● ● ● ● ● ● ● ● ● ● ● ● ● ● ● ●

There is no Cosmic Two-By-Four. Please read that sentence again! One more time. Thank you. There is no Cosmic Two-By-Four—pine, oak, treated lumber, galactic laser beam, or otherwise. Since there is truly only One Power and One Presence in the universe, God the Good, this "wooden" phrase goes against the grain of the oldest and most revered Truth Principles. We do not believe God, the Good, punishes us with two-by-fours, wooden paddles, willow sticks, baseball bats, or any other "wooden explanations."

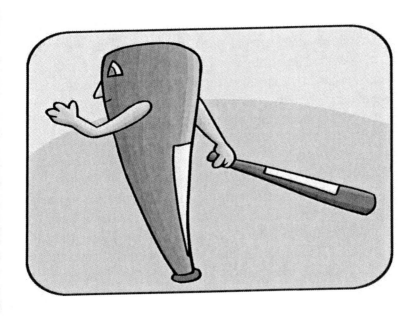

HIT BY A COSMIC TWO-BY-FOUR

Truth Triage

The purely human, not cosmic, two-by-four is in our own hands! It is our poor decisions and errant actions that punish us and hurt us, not God. As long as we keep making bad decisions we will keep getting bad results. A 2x4 moment is an opportunity to experience an "aha;" however, we can keep creating 2x4 moments if we neglect to learn from our experiences.

"Aha's" are the result of a change in perspective, an insight which comes from an intuitive leap in consciousness. Two-by-four moments occur when we suddenly realize that our own stale thought patterns and belief systems are no longer valid. If we keep beating ourselves up with the metaphorical 2x4, perhaps it's time to pause and reflect on the thoughts, choices, and actions we've taken which lead to our self-flagellation. This awareness is an *inside-out* realization.

REPLACEMENT PHRASE

• •

I've Created

a 2x4

Moment

What This Phrase Assumes

The Law of Mind Action states that thoughts held in mind produce after their kind. In other words, if we are thinking negative thoughts then the next thought will most likely be negative. If we are thinking positive thoughts then the next thought will most likely be positive. This is frequently believed to mean that every thought we hold in our mind and concentrate on through our thinking and feelings, produces after its kind in the material world.

GET OVER IT!

● ●

This is too literal of an interpretation. It over-simplifies a complex and dynamic Truth Principle. This myopic view of the Law of Mind Action can lead people astray. It creates a "pulling rabbits out of the hat" mentality. People tend to believe that each thought they have produces something in the "real" world. People can become overly fearful of their own thoughts. While it is important for each and every one of us to watch our thoughts, we must not be afraid to think! Otherwise, we will turn mind action into mime action. The Law of Mind Action involves inner consequences and potential outer consequences, as much as it does the actual thoughts which produce those consequences.

THOUGHTS HELD IN MIND PRODUCE AFTER THEIR KIND   15

Truth Triage

While all thoughts have their effects, we need not be fearful of our thoughts. It is true that the thoughts we hold with our thinking and feeling natures can be more powerful than just passing thoughts and feelings. While all of our thoughts are based on Divine Ideas, thoughts formed and influenced by our outer senses are said to be formative. That is, they help shape, develop, and mold our human experience. Thoughts based on Divine Ideas are said to be creative. Let's look at this on several levels:

At the Level of Consciousness

Thoughts we hold in mind tend to produce after their kind at the level of our evolving human consciousness *almost* 100% of the time. It can't be 100% of the time because if it were 100% of the time we would never be able to change our thoughts or minds! However, every thought we hold will most likely produce after its kind until we change our thinking and feeling.

At the Level of the Body

Recent medical science has pretty much proven that our minds and bodies are hard wired. Every thought we hold has an effect on our bodies. Happy thoughts give rise to happy molecules; unhappy thoughts give rise to unhappy molecules. Unhappy thoughts suppress the immune system; happy thoughts boost the immune system. Simply and briefly, this is how our mind, our consciousness, can affect our health.

At the Level of the Outer Realm

At the level of the outer realm (material world), our "thought power" can manifest anywhere from 100% to not at all. Whenever we make a decision to do something, it happens first at the level of the mind. Once it is in the mind, it comes to life at the level of consciousness. At this point we have a powerful choice to make! We decide if and how we are actually going to go about creating that thought in the real world. And assuming we do decide to take it to the outer realm, there are a multitude of forms the thought can take.

So thoughts held in mind **can** produce after their kind in the outer realm, but they do not always do so. Many of the thoughts we hold seem to have no visible effect. It is up to us whether or not we transform those thoughts into manifestation.

REPLACEMENT
PHRASE

• • • • • • • • • • • • • • • • • • •

Thoughts & Feelings
Held in Consciousness
Create in
Consciousness

What This Phrase Assumes

Many people who are unfamiliar with this law's True Nature assume that through our thoughts, attention, and intentions we attract (draw to us) anything we want—a new BMW or Mercedes, a 5,000 square foot home, our soul mate, a huge HD TV, the perfect toaster, the parking place nearest the front door of a retail store, etc. People also assume that we attract everything which happens to us.

GET OVER IT!

● ●

We can become overly weary or fearful about what we are attracting into our lives just because of a simple thought we have.

*Here's a down-to-earth way of explaining the Law of Attraction. It's not what most people think it is! Mentally, we do not attract **things**. Depending on our "thought atmosphere" (negative or positive thoughts or intentions), we build a thought climate which leads to positive choices and actions, or negative choices and actions ~ either of which lead to certain outcomes.*

I ATTRACTED THIS TO ME

Truth Triage

What is actually happening here is more about perception and less about attraction. What we believe, we tend to see. It is really about how we are "sorting" and seeing all the data that is coming at us. Imagine that you decide to buy a new Volkswagen Beetle automobile. What happens? As you drive around town you begin to see Volkswagen Beetles wherever you go.

It's not that you are attracting them to you. It's not that there is a God or a universe "out there" arranging more of these vehicles for you to see. It is simply that Volkswagen Beetles are on your mind because you intend to purchase one. This results in your sorting all the incoming data differently than you did prior to making the decision to buy the Beetle. All the Volkswagen Beetles on the road are suddenly *more visible* to you because you decided to buy one. They are on your *Beetle radar.* You have suddenly become more aware of them. It's not that Volkswagen Beetles are attracted to you; you are attracted to them by your choices and perceptions.

REPLACEMENT
PHRASE

• •

I Attracted Myself to This

What This Phrase Assumes

How many times have you heard this one? This self-declaration implies that there is something outside of us that is pre-determining where we are supposed to be. People subscribing to this philosophy put their own instincts and sense of direction on hold, believing that something or someone "out there" has specifically designed an "experiential gauntlet" for them so they won't stray too far from what they're supposed to do!

GET OVER IT!

• •

Stop shoulding on yourself! Who or what says you're where you're supposed to be? The Truth is you are where you ARE. And you are where you are because of the choices you've made and the actions you've taken. To give someone or something else credit for your being where you are is being too modest, or too naive, or just plain gullible.

There is no God "out there," separate from us, that is pre-determining our lives. God, Spirit, the Truth (whatever name you give to the Ultimate Oneness) does not have an individualized, predetermined, tactical plan for your life or anyone else's. Our overall direction is our own spiritual unfoldment. And that direction is the same for all of us. We are here to express as much Good and as much Christ Consciousness as we can, based on the level of our consciousness, awareness, and growth.

I am Here!

I'M RIGHT WHERE I'M SUPPOSED TO BE 29

Truth Triage

We are right where we are as a result of our own thoughts, feelings beliefs, and choices. There is no external pre-determining force. That would be a farce. We are not puppets moved about by a micro-managing puppeteer. We are right where we are because we are *us being us at the point of us*. In that sense there is nowhere else we can be, unless we're beside ourselves because we're upset about something. And that subject is outside the scope of this book—we know our limits.

At the risk of repeating ourselves—and boring you—we want to wrap this small treatise up by saying, rather emphatically, that you are where you are because where you are is the result of *your* choices and *your* right of consciousness.

REPLACEMENT
PHRASE

• •

I'm Right Where
I Choose
To Be

What This Phrase Assumes

If we want to do something we don't believe we can do or is not part of our personal makeup, then we may tend to rationalize that our best course of action is to fake it till we make it. Faking it, we assume, will allow us the time we need to create the outcome we want.

GET OVER IT!

●●●●●●●●●●●●●●●●●●●

*While this is a cute phrase, it is a dangerous and corrosive statement. The problem with this type of pathological, yes pathological, reasoning is that it assumes pretense is a virtue. It champions fakery, deceit, and counterfeit logic as success strategies. It implies we don't have the present wherewithal (skills, education, and expertise) to manifest our desires. To make things even more dangerous, this type of thinking results in people feeling like frauds, eroding self worth. This is definitely **not** the kind of consciousness we want to manifest!*

FAKE IT TILL YOU MAKE IT   35

Truth Triage

The mere decision to fake it may be based on some kernel of Truth or belief we already have. In this sense, we might be faking 99% while the authentic 1% of us knows we are, in fact, faking it. Essentially, in that moment, we are choosing to live from the 1% instead of the 99%. Therefore, we may tell ourselves we are not entirely faking it.

For example, if you are not feeling as happy as you'd like to be, instead of faking happiness, take a serious look at your current happiness report card. Your decision to be happier is proof that there is a small, unrecognized, part of you that is already happy. That part is not faking it. Focusing on being happy makes it grow in your awareness and consciousness.

Faking it comes from a *sand castle* position, one which is easily washed away by tides of doubt, fear, unworthiness, and any number of self-deceptive tactics. On the other hand, *FAITHING IT UNTIL YOU MAKE IT* is based on the solid rock of *indivisibleness*. Faith implies *knowing* something is true in spite of outer appearances; fakery implies *no-ing*.

REPLACEMENT
PHRASE

• •

*Faith It Till
You Make It*

What This Phrase Assumes

Divine Order is one of the most misunderstood New Thought concepts. It is most often used in the traditional sense that there is a God outside of us ordering everything that happens in the universe, including our daily lives. The idea is that there is a set order for our lives and that all of our activities are governed by it.

GET OVER IT!

• • • • • • • • • • • • • • • • • • • •

Most people get Divine Order out-of-order! There is no such thing as Divine Order as we ordinarily use it. This idea has been poorly understood and misused over the years. This phrase is used more as a statement of resignation rather than the statement of power it is meant to be.

*In his book, **The Twelve Powers**, Charles Fillmore, co-founder of Unity, defined Divine Order in the following way:*

> "[We] can never exercise dominion until [we] know who and what [we are] and, knowing, bring forth that knowledge into the external by exercising it in Divine Order, which is mind, idea, and manifestation." *(Pg 113)*

It is clear that Charles Fillmore did not see Divine Order as a divine fiat or divine proclamation. He saw it as a Divine Process, a point of power. In other Fillmore writings we learn that everything is based on a Divine Idea and everything comes into expression through the process of Mind-Idea-Expression (Divine Order). It is a universal process.

DIVINE ORDER

Truth Triage

If everything is brought into manifestation through this Divine process, then we can use this process as a point of power. Make sense? Think about it. We can claim Divine Order at any moment because Divine Order is not an event. It is a process which is always present and always available. Any effects we are experiencing now are the result of being Divinely Ordered (Remember Divine Order is Mind, Idea, Expression). More importantly, if there is a present effect we do not like, we can choose to put a new cause into motion through the process of Divinely Ordering our experience. In a sense, whenever we claim Divine Order we are saying that our current experience is the result of the process of Divine Order. What's more, we can change our next experience using that same Divine Ordering process.

It is not that God "out there" is Divinely Ordering events (effects). God is the process Itself we use to bring about effects (events). We can Divinely Order our experience or mis-order our experiences. It's up to us.

REPLACEMENT PHRASE

● ●

I'm Divinely Ordering

What This Phrase Assumes

What this phrase means to most people is that there is a God "out there" waving a magic wand making sure everything works on our behalf all the time for good results. The implication is that we are shepherded through life's experiences by a benevolent Presence who guarantees safe passage through every experience even if those experiences are considered bad experiences. There seems to be an element of predictable good associated with this assumption.

Here is scriptural justification from Romans 8:26-28 *(American Standard Bible)*:

> *Likewise the Spirit helps us in our weakness: for we do not know how to pray as we ought, but that very Spirit intercedes with sighs too deep for words. And God, who searches the heart, knows what is the mind of Spirit, because the Spirit intercedes for the saints according to the will of God.*
>
> *We know that all things work together for good for those who love God, who are called according to his purpose.*

Here is how the same verse reads in *The Message: The Bible in Contemporary Language*:

> *He knows us far better than we know ourselves, knows our pregnant condition, and keeps us present before God. That's why we can be so sure that every detail in our lives of love for God is worked into something good.*

GET OVER IT!

● ● ● ● ● ● ● ● ● ● ● ● ● ● ● ● ● ● ●

*There is no God "out there" waving a magic wand, or anything else for that matter, which guarantees everything will turn out right. Stuff happens in life. Sometimes rather disturbing stuff. You know what we mean. The Truth is it is up to **us** to engineer goodness into our human experiences from our Christ Natures.*

ALL THINGS WORK TOGETHER FOR GOOD   47

Truth Triage

This phrase is actually an affirmation of what is possible. There is a Rightness that is the Truth of us, which knows how to use everything for good if we so choose. We are sure you've noticed by now that we humans always have the free will to choose selfishness or selflessness, make self-centered choices or other-centered choices, and choose Truth over error.

Eric Butterworth captured the essence of this idea in his book, *Unity: A Quest for Truth*, when he said, "The great need is not to set things right, but to see them rightly."

REPLACEMENT PHRASE

. . . .

I Work All Things
Together for Good

8

We Are the Light of the World

What This Phrase Assumes

This is a phrase based on Biblical scripture. Jesus said, "You are the light of the world. A city built on a hill cannot be hid" (Matt.5:14, New Revised Standard Version).

Here's another way to put it: "You're here to be light, bringing out the God-colors in the world. God is not a secret to be kept. We're going public with this, as public as a city on a hill" (Matt. 5:14, The Message).

Many believe this to mean that we are somehow light or light beings come to illumine the world with our light.

GET OVER IT!

• •

Let us put some light on the subject. This phrase is not intended to be taken literally. It is meant to be taken metaphorically. We are not literally light or light beings. This "light" means awareness, understanding, and illumination, as in illuminating the mind. Scripture tells us that we are created in the "image and likeness" of God.

Since God is Spirit (not light) we, too, are Spirit. Did you ever notice God said, "Let there by light" on the first day, and then created the sun and the moon on the fourth day? Since God said, "Let there be light," it strongly suggests that God (Cause) precedes light (understanding), which makes light an effect. Because we are Spirit, we both precede and make light (awareness, understanding, illumination) possible.

Truth Triage

The Message states it well: "Taken metaphysically, light means understanding and illumination. Then, when we say we are light, we are truly saying that we are [awareness], understanding, and illumination at some level of our being."

More importantly, because we are Spirit, we can bring that understanding and illumination to any situation, experience, and aspect of our lives.

REPLACEMENT PHRASE

• •

We Illuminate
the World

#9
Divine
Appointment/
Divine Timing

What This Phrase Assumes

The phrase "Divine Appointment" is frequently used when two or more people find themselves connected by what seems to be a heaven-ordained occasion. Divine Timing describes an event which seems miraculous. These two phrases are also used to describe desired outcomes which happen because they are in sync with Divine Timing, making them much like the reasoning used to explain Divine Order. These phrases are used more from a point of resignation, accepting the wisdom or whims of an external Divine Will. The underlying thought is that what we want to happen will happen when God wills it and in God's own timing.

GET OVER IT!

● ●

While this may be a comforting idea, it suggests that Divine Appointments and Divine Timing are imposed, predetermined arrangements by some cosmic being "out there." This, like so many of our New Thought sayings, implies that there is a Power or Presence in the universe that imposes its own timing and causes things to happen in a predetermined, appointed way which negates our power of self-determined choice. From our contrarian perspective, although this One Power and One Presence is the Truth of all of us, It does not, would not, and cannot have a predetermined plan or timing-orientation because at Its level of being there is no time, which means there is no planning to be done.

Truth Triage

Most of us have no doubt had experiences which seemed like Divine Appointments because everything felt just right. We believe this has more to do with One Mindedness. It is not that this One Mind is willing, intending, or predetermining anything. It is more that there is an Omnipresent Knowingness of which we are a part, and from this One-Minding, we create experiences that are Divinely Timed by us.

REPLACEMENT PHRASE

● ● ● ● ● ● ● ● ● ● ● ● ● ● ● ● ● ● ● ●

One-Minding

Creates

Divine Timing

What This Phrase Assumes

This phrase is used much like Divine Timing and Divine Appointment. It implies that everything is happening just as it is supposed to happen. And what is supposed to happen is determined by God, since (according to this assumption) God has a specific plan for each and every one of us!

GET OVER IT!

• •

This is another example of the One Power and One Presence being misinterpreted to mean that It has a specific, tactical, micro-managed plan, for each and everyone of us. The plan—please read this slowly and deliberately—the plan is for us to fulfill our Christhood. That's it! The thoughts, intentions, choices, and actions we take getting there are our tactical, self-determined moves to become the Christs we're meant to be!

NOTHING HAPPENS BY ACCIDENT

Truth Triage

Well, of course, **nothing** happens by accident. And it is not because an external God is predetermining everything. How many people take time during a normal day's experience to wonder how they literally got to the present moment in which they find themselves? It's like finding oneself in a particular classroom, or on a specific park bench, or at a restaurant and all of a sudden saying, "Oh, wow! I'm in this classroom, or on this bench, or on this chair. How'd that happen? A minute ago I was drinking my coffee, tea, or water at home and, whoosh, here I am!"

We are where we are because of the individual choices we make and the actions we take. And our job is to choose to transform every situation into a meaningful growth experience.

REPLACEMENT PHRASE

• •

Everything
Happens by
Intent

What This Phrase Assumes

This phrase is frequently used when we look back on a situation or an event that was painful, unexpected, or life-changing. It is frequently used when people look back on a diagnosis of cancer, HIV/AIDS, heart attack, or other health challenges. People use it when they look back on divorce, unemployment, relocation, an accident, or some other untoward event which they believe caused their life to be enhanced, deepened, or fulfilled in some way.

GET OVER IT!

• •

In and of themselves, things, events, and situations do not bless us because they are not causative. Let this statement sink in before you continue. They are simply what they are—occurrences! No more, no less. When we look back on an untoward event in our lives and say, "it blessed me" we are misattributing the blessing. There is no God "out there" wanting us to go through an event or situation so we can be blessed by it, in order to learn the lesson it was sent to teach us. That kind of reasoning is both disempowering and self-defeating. It implies that events have the power to cause a reaction or response in us.

IT BLESSED ME

Truth Triage

The key is how we USE events or situations. Everyone, upon looking back on an event, can certainly find a blessing as a result of the experience. However, blessings are more about what we DO with events. The event itself did not cause the blessing that came forth. If events were causative of blessings, then every same, or similar, event would cause the same, or similar, blessing for everyone.

We know that some people use a diagnosis of cancer, for example, to get depressed and decide not to be proactive about their lives or the cancer treatment. And, so, perhaps they may die sooner than they might have. Another person may use the same diagnosis to be proactive about their treatment and live a fuller life. Some people use the event as a trigger to research the disease so they can learn more about that particular cancer. This decision—not the event—is what blesses the person and others. It is what we CHOOSE to do with the event that causes the blessing. The events we encounter do not bless us; we bless ourselves, and perhaps others, by the way we respond to what happens to us.

REPLACEMENT
PHRASE
• •

I Blessed It

12

What We
Resist
Persists

What This Phrase Assumes

Whatever we give our energy to tends to persist. The underlying assumption is not to resist anything we want out of our lives. If we resist it, it will stay even longer.

GET OVER IT!

● ●

This idea is taken much too literally, especially with regards to outer events. This type of reasoning can be very disempowering and keep us from being proactive in our lives.

For example, someone who does not resist his or her spousal abuse simply remains in a relationship where more and more abuse will probably occur.

WHAT WE RESIST PERSISTS

77

Truth Triage

This saying is true at the level of our conscious awareness. It is based on the Law of Mind Action: thoughts held in mind produce after their kind ... or as we like to say, thoughts and feelings held in consciousness create in consciousness. The idea is that the thoughts we hold in consciousness—the thoughts to which we give our attention and energy—grow in their effect and importance. It follows that thoughts which we resist are given our attention and energy, and therefore grow in our awareness as well; thus, they persist even longer than if we had simply let them go.

When we meditate, for example, it is best to allow intruding thoughts to pass unchallenged through our conscious awareness. Otherwise, they will camp out in our minds and pollute our meditative experience.

REPLACEMENT PHRASE

• •

What We Resist in Mind Stays in Mind

WHAT WE RESIST PERSISTS

13

Birds of a Feather
Flock Together /
Opposites Attract

What This Phrase Assumes

We're going to give you a bird's eye view of these two assumptions which we believe are flying out of formation. These two phrases have been winging it for a long time. People assume, stereotypically, that like-minded individuals are naturally attracted to each other, as if there is a "nesting" quality to their relationship. (Bear with us. We're having fun with the analogy.)

And as far as opposites attracting, this logic assumes there is an automatic, incontrovertible, mindless magnetism that pulls people together. You're probably already catching on to our dissatisfaction with these two old familiar phrases.

GET OVER IT!

● ●

Sounds like fowl play to us! People choose to flock or not to flock. It doesn't matter if the person is like you or the opposite from you.

BIRDS OF A FEATHER FLOCK TOGETHER /
OPPOSITES ATTRACT

Truth Triage

Its not about whether we attract or what we attract. And the point isn't whether birds of a feather flock together or whether opposites attract. It's about what we do with the birds and opposites that come our way.

It is within our power to identify with flocks, herds, schools, or colonies—or NOT! Our associations or dis-associations are our choice. It is our calling to express as much Goodness, and Godness, and Christ Consciousness that we possibly can.

REPLACEMENT PHRASE

• •

We Choose
Who We
Flock With

BIRDS OF A FEATHER FLOCK TOGETHER /
OPPOSITES ATTRACT

What This Phrase Assumes

This metaphor is used to illustrate the relationship of God to us and us to God. It suggests that while a drop of the ocean contains all the elements of the ocean it is not the entire ocean. It assumes we are a tiny little piece of God Stuff.

GET OVER IT!

● ●

This metaphor, like all metaphors, breaks down at a certain point. Since the drop can be removed from the ocean we assume that we can be removed from God. (Is that where the phrase 'drop in the bucket' comes from? We're playing with you.) There is no such thing as a piece of God!

WE ARE LIKE A DROP IN THE OCEAN

Truth Triage

This metaphor is great in that it gets across the idea that we are essentially God stuff. Each of us contains all the qualities of God—not some of them and not part of them, all of them. Since God is everywhere present, all of God is present everywhere. This is hard to comprehend from our three dimensional standpoint and yet it is true.

This is summed up beautifully by Charles Fillmore in his book, *Christian Healing*:

> *"Individual consciousness is like an eddy in the ocean ~ all the elements that are found in the ocean are also found in the eddy, and every eddy may, in due course, receive and give forth all that is in the ocean."*

REPLACEMENT
PHRASE

• • • • • • • • • • • • • • • • • • •

The Allness of the Ocean
is the Eachness
of Its Droplets

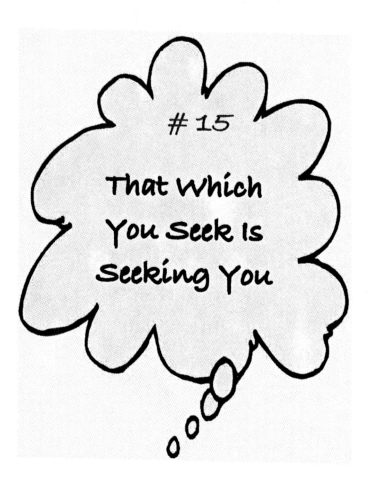

What This Phrase Assumes

This phrase assumes that because we are seeking God, God is seeking us.

GET OVER IT!

● ●

*Although this 'sense-seeking missile' smacks of separation, it hides a kernel of Truth. Since we are "created in the image and likeness of God" (you may want to **seek** your favorite Bible translation to confirm our paraphrase), that which we seek we already are. Seeking for anything implies distance and separation.*

Ernest Holmes said it quite eloquently when he wrote, "The thing we are looking for is the thing we are looking with." (Science of Divine Mind, p. 364).

THAT WHICH YOU SEEK IS SEEKING YOU

Truth Triage

What is helpful about this phrase is that it reinforces the idea that God is involved in our seeking. As we become aware of our Goodness, our "Godness" becomes self-evident. When we realize that the 'k' in seeking stands for **knowing** that *what we seek we already are,* we turn **seeking** into **seeing** the Truth of us. And the Truth is we are God at the point of us!

REPLACEMENT PHRASE

● ● ● ● ● ● ● ● ● ● ● ● ● ● ● ● ● ● ●

That Which You Seek,
You Already Are

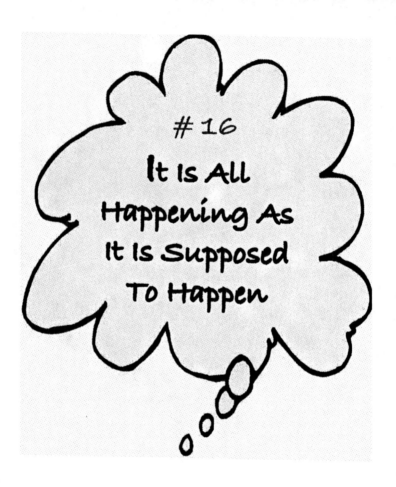

98

What This Phrase Assumes

According to this assumption whatever is happening is part of a predetermined plan and will. Even if we do not like what is happening, it is our job to deal with it because there is some bigger reason or plan that we do not understand or know.

GET OVER IT!

• •

There IS no external force or plan being imposed upon us by a micro-managing Cosmic Deity. We are the masters of our lives and have dominion over all of our thoughts, intentions, choices, and actions. Please read that last sentence again so it soaks in. Again please! One more time.

See, you were **supposed** to re-read it. No you weren't. You **chose** to re-read it—three times—at our insistence.

We're messing with you!

Truth Triage

There is a kernel of Truth here. The speck of Truth is that there *is* a Divine Will and Plan. However, it is non-specific for any of our lives and circumstances. The God-Will and the God-Plan are for each of us to express the maximum amount of Goodness, the maximum amount of Godness, and the maximum amount of Christ Consciousness we are at our present level of consciousness. All of us have an inner urge to express more and more good. It's in our spiritual DNA! Each of us, through our choices and free will, determines how we outpicture Goodness, "God-ness," Christ Consciousness.

REPLACEMENT PHRASE

● ● ● ● ● ● ● ● ● ● ● ● ● ● ● ● ● ● ● ●

Whatever Happens,
I Choose To Use
For Good

IT IS ALL HAPPENING AS IT IS SUPPOSED TO HAPPEN 103

What This Phrase Assumes

Whatever one sees on the outside is an out-picturing of what is on the inside. Whatever you can identify in another is somehow a part of you.

GET OVER IT!

• •

Mirror, mirror on the wall. Who's the most gullible of them all?

This concept has become magnified into magical proportions. It is taken much too literally.

LIFE IS A MIRROR

Truth Triage

This can be a useful concept, but it has its troublesome limitations. What we identify with in another TENDS to be that part of us we project onto another, if we have a strong emotional reaction coming along with it. For example, it could mean *a kettle calling another kettle black* (i.e., a thief calling another thief a thief.) However, suppose we witness someone stealing and thus call the person a thief. That does not necessarily mean we are a thief, too.

Now, if the person identifying the thief has an unusually high emotional reaction, it may call for a little self-examination to see if he or she possesses any personal characteristics of a thief—whatever they are.

The Truth we want to emphasize here is that life is not a mirror. The world of appearance is more like a mirage, an illusion that appears real, but is not. We have the power to transform the illusory world of appearance into a solid reality of Truth.

REPLACEMENT
PHRASE

• •

Life Is a
Mirage

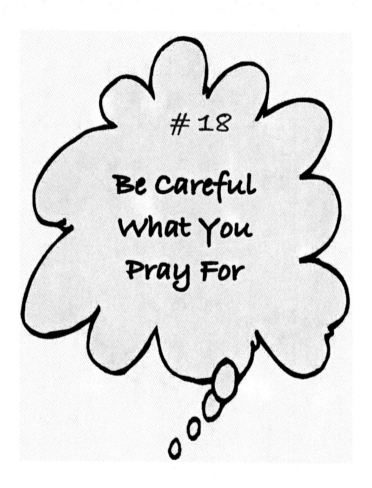

18

Be Careful What You Pray For

What This Phrase Assumes

Carefully concocted, this phrase is taken to magical levels. The idea is that when we pray for something, we'd better really be specific or we may get something we really don't want. An example might be a person praying for a new partner, or a new car, or a new job and not being specific enough. The person may get a partner, or the car, or the job, but the partner may have unwanted qualities, the car payment strains the budget, or the job is on the other side of the country.

GET OVER IT!

• •

This phrase, although well-meaning, is simply taken entirely too literally. It is not useful to build fear and guilt around prayer. That's not the purpose of prayer. Prayer is experiencing the Oneness of "Godness," not something which you should be fearful of practicing.

BE CAREFUL WHAT YOU PRAY FOR

Truth Triage

When we pray, we are coming to the awareness of our Oneness in God/Spirit, and there is no reason to attach any fear to our prayers. We pray affirmatively, knowing we are One Divine Substance. In affirmative prayer, we do not pray "to God out there," but rather we pray "from the awareness of Oneness."

The point of prayer is not the goodies we get, but the Goodness we realize we are!

REPLACEMENT PHRASE

● ●

Pray From the
Awareness
of Oneness

19

Things Happen in Their Own Time

What This Phrase Assumes

    People who use this phrase assume there is a Divine Timing that we have no clue about. Therefore, the reasoning goes, we must be patient and wait until the imposed timing is right. This same thought is expressed as "It will happen when it is supposed to."

GET OVER IT!

● ●

The sayings "Things happen in their own time" or "It will happen when it is supposed to" imply there is an external force or presence that dictates, imposes, and controls everything. The Truth is, things don't happen in THEIR own time—as if things had a will of their own. Things happen when individuals decide they happen.

THINGS HAPPEN IN THEIR OWN TIME

Truth Triage

Since the One Power and One Presence is the Truth of us, (you do believe in only One Power, God the Good, don't you?), we have the power, wisdom, and intelligence to Divinely Time our actions. There is no thing external to us which determines the timing. We determine when, what, how, and where things happen.

REPLACEMENT PHRASE

• •

Things Happen
in Our
Own Time

What This Phrase Assumes

It doesn't take a rocket scientist or a fortune teller to see what these phrases have in common: There is an implication of an external God, separate from us, who can and does talk to us, and who can perform actions as us, without our involvement or consent.

GET OVER IT!

● ● ● ● ● ● ● ● ● ● ● ● ● ● ● ● ● ● ● ●

God is not an eternal, external anthropomorphic Being who uses a cosmic megaphone to get our attention. We invite you to give that some conscientious, prayerful thought. Also, we're going to be adamant about this: we invite you to be willing to forget everything traditional you learned about a God "out there." We're not kidding! Two thousand years of embedded, dogmatic theology has gotten millions of people to look "out there" for a God which is indivisibly the very essence of us.

While the One Power and One Presence is said to be transcendent and immanent, we experience the Sacred at the point of us. That means the infiniteness of God is in the seeming finiteness of us. Since Spirit, God, is us, then the Divine guidance is coming from us.

Truth Triage

God is not externally talking to us. Have we said that already? The two commonly used phrases we are taking issue with continue to perpetuate the illusion of our separation from Spirit. Worse, "God told me" indirectly affirms that the *me of us* (our personality) is the real me which is separate from God/Spirit. At the risk of sounding judgmental, nothing could be further from Truth.

We want to make this perfectly clear. We believe people *do* experience a Guiding Presence or Voice; however, it doesn't come to them or through them—it comes FROM them. This Guiding Presence is the Higher Self, the God-Self. We can add more amperage to our spiritual capacity by becoming the best Christs we can be at our current level of consciousness. And we can do this by claiming *this* Voice as *our* True Voice.

REPLACEMENT PHRASE

• •

It was My
God Essence;
my Christ-Nature
Revealed

21

It's All Good;
It's All God

What This Phrase Assumes

This phrase assumes that everything we see, touch, feel, and experience is God, and regardless of how it seems to be, it is good. This phrase implies that on a human level, everything happening, such as health challenges, poverty, violence, and wars, is all good.

GET OVER IT!

● ●

Everything isn't good, isn't God, and isn't intended by God. We're simply going to repeat that statement: Everything isn't good, isn't God, and isn't intended by God.

Truth Triage

This troublesome perspective stems from the idea that God is everywhere present. Unfortunately many truly spiritual people make the erroneous jump to the idea that since God is everywhere present, then everything must be God, and therefore must be good.

Since God is everywhere present, then this Presence that is the True Self is available so that we can Divinely Order whatever is presently in our lives. This Omnipresence becomes a point of power within us when we claim Oneness. Calling all situations good is not saying that events, in and of themselves, are good. What it is saying is that situations can be used for good and that we can look for creative ways to make them good.

REPLACEMENT
PHRASE

● ● ● ● ● ● ● ● ● ● ● ● ● ● ● ● ● ● ● ●

It's All Good when
I Remember
I'm God

What This Phrase Assumes

This phrase is used in classes, sermons, and counseling sessions to mean that we must determine if what is being taught is true for the "human" us.

GET OVER IT!

• •

Our personalities (egos) do not like change. To the ego/personality, anything and everything new feels funny when it doesn't fit existing beliefs. So it doesn't resonate with the approved parameters of the status quo. Therefore, we end up walking away from a teaching or a Truth Principle when there is something of value for us. Sounds absurd, doesn't it? But people do it every day.

New Ideas

TAKE WHAT FITS / WORKS / RESONATES
AND LEAVE THE REST

Truth Triage

This phrase was never intended to be used from the level of the personality. As originally taught, this well-meaning advice was intended for us to take the teaching or Principle to our Higher Self in the Silence. In this way our True Nature, our Christ Self, determines what is good for us.

REPLACEMENT PHRASE

• •

Take It To the
Silence

23

It's Synchronicity

What This Phrase
Assumes

The way in which this "mysteriously" sounding word is used is more like magic and is used with a sense of wonder. This phrase assumes that, once again, God as the master chess player in the sky, is manipulating events and people so that they come together in inexplicable ways.

GET OVER IT!

• •

Well, we think we have pretty much beaten the drum silly over the idea that there is not a God "out there" manipulating events and people to create synchronistic events or anything else. This idea once again puts all of us at the "mercy" and the power of an external God. And, might we add, a whimsical God that makes these synchronistic events happen in one moment and not happen in another.

IT'S SYNCHRONICITY

Truth Triage

As usual, there is a wonderful kernel of Truth in this statement. It reminds us of the Oneness that is the Truth that underlies everything. It is interesting that we are surprised when these events occur, when we really should be surprised when they don't happen.

The online site, *Wikipedia*, has this to say[1]: "Synchronous events reveal an underlying pattern, a conceptual framework which encompasses, but is larger than, any of the systems which display the synchronicity. ... Carl Jung coined the word to describe what he called 'temporally coincident occurrences of acausal events.' Jung variously described synchronicity as an 'acausal connecting principle' ... It was a principle Jung felt gave conclusive evidence for his concepts of archetypes and the collective unconscious, in that it was descriptive of a governing dynamic that underlaid the whole of human experience and history—social, emotional, psychological, and spiritual."

Wow! That's some heavy stuff for such a simple word like *synchronicity*. And there are doubters. In fact, here is some more interesting information from *The Skeptics Dictionary*[2]:

---

[1]http://en.wikipedia.org/wiki/Synchronicity
[2]http://skepdic.com/jung.html

"What reasons are there for accepting synchronicity as an explanation for anything in the real world? What it explains is more simply and elegantly explained by the ability of the human mind to find meaning and significance where there is none (apophenia). ... However, if you think of all the pairs of things that can happen in a person's lifetime, and add to that our very versatile ability of finding meaningful connections between things, it then seems likely that most of us will experience many meaningful coincidences. Coincidences are predictable, but we are the ones who give them meaning."

Just in case you are curious, *Apophenia* is the spontaneous perception of connections and meaningfulness of unrelated phenomena.

We think we can combine both of these points of view and arrive at a very satisfying and EMPOWERING view of synchronicity.

First, there is "One-mindedness" operating, even if it is primarily through the collective unconsciousness, collective consciousness, or as our early writers called it, race consciousness.

Further, the entry from *The Skeptics Dictionary* makes the very important point of how we relate unrelated events within our own minds by the thoughts, beliefs and attitudes we hold.

REPLACEMENT
PHRASE

● ● ● ● ● ● ● ● ● ● ● ● ● ● ● ● ● ● ● ●

I Synchronize!

#24

It Is

What It Is

What This Phrase Assumes

This phrase assumes that whatever is happening in our life is what is happening in our life! And it prompts us to rationalize that we might as well just get used to it just the way it is. This phrase is frequently linked to the idea that everything is happening as it is supposed to be happening.

GET OVER IT!

● ●

Yes, what it is, it is—*AND, that is not the end of it. We do not have to stay stuck with what we have, just because it is what it is. Nor are things happening as they are supposed to. This type of thinking keeps us stuck and mired in the continuing abdication of our personal power.*

Truth Triage

The Truth is that whatever *IS* in our life is affected by what we name it or call it. We have dominion (control) over whatever is in our lives and especially what is in our minds through the power of our minds. If we call something bad then we treat it bad and go about finding more reasons why it is bad. If we call something good then we go about finding good in it or creating good out of the situation. This places the power where it has always been—and always will be—at the point of us.

REPLACEMENT PHRASE

• •

It Is What
I Call It

What This Phrase Assumes

This stream of consciousness perspective assumes a flow that is really a flow of God Consciousness. It implies that sometimes we are in the flow and sometimes we are not. When we are in the flow, life goes smoothly and miraculously. Synchronistic events occur. When we are not in the flow, things do not go smoothly. We seem to bump aimlessly along through life, confusing activity with accomplishment.

GET OVER IT!

● ●

There is a "seeming flow" in life, and we can never be separated from it—because WE ARE THE FLOW.

Truth Triage

Yes, there does seem to be a sense of Truth in the idea that sometimes it feels like life is just flowing along, with everything falling perfectly in place, while at other times it feels like nothing is working and life is difficult.

The Truth is that our Christ Nature is the Truth of what we are. It is the very Flow of all that is. As we emphatically mentioned previously, we are the flow. When we feel we are not in the flow, it is nothing more than a state of mind, attitude, or awareness. It is not a statement of fact and Truth. We can never NOT be the flow. (We doubled up on the negative to make a point. It just seemed to flow off our pens!)

In his book, *In the Flow of Life*, Eric Butterworth says: "The light you seek is not somewhere else, but where you are. Don't ask God to guide you or beg God to make the choice for you. Instead, affirm that you are in the flow of light, and God is the light. **You are in it. It is in you. It is the reality of you.** It is not something to reach for but a Truth to accept." (p. 75)

REPLACEMENT PHRASE

● ● ● ● ● ● ● ● ● ● ● ● ● ● ● ● ● ●

I Am

the Flow

I'M IN THE FLOW / I'M NOT IN THE FLOW   159

SUMMARY CHART

GET OVER IT	INSTEAD, SAY:
#1. Hit by a Cosmic 2x4	I've created a 2x4 moment
#2. Thoughts held in mind produce after their own kind.	Thoughts and feelings held in consciousness create in consciousness.
#3. I attracted this to me.	I attracted myself to this.
#4. I'm right where I'm supposed to be.	I'm right where I choose to be.
#5. Fake it till you make it.	Faith it till you make it.
#6. Divine Order	I'm Divinely Ordering
#7. All things work together for good.	I work all things together for good.
#8. We are the light of the world.	We illuminate the world.
#9. Divine Appointment/ Divine Timing	One-Minding Creates Divine Timing
#10. Nothing happens by accident.	Everything happens by intent.
#11. It blessed me.	I blessed it.

GET OVER IT!	INSTEAD, SAY:
#12. What we resist, persists.	What we resist in mind stays in mind.
#13. Birds of a feather flock together/Opposites attract.	We choose who we flock with.
#14. We are like a drop in the ocean.	The allness of the ocean is in the eachness of its droplets.
#15. That which you seek is seeking you.	That which you seek, you already are.
#16. It's all happening as it is supposed to happen.	Whatever happens I choose to use for good.
#17. Life is a mirror.	Life is a mirage.
#18. Be careful what you pray for.	Pray from the awareness of Oneness.
#19. Things happen in their own time.	Things happen in our own time.
#20. It wasn't me; it was Spirit/God told me.	It was my God Essence; my Christ Nature revealed.
#21. It's all good; it's all God.	It's all good when I remember I'm God.

GET OVER IT!	INSTEAD, SAY:
#22. Take what fits/works/ resonates and leave the rest.	Take it to the Silence.
#23. It's synchronicity.	I synchronize!
#24. It is what it is.	It is what I call it.
#25. I'm in the flow/I'm not in the flow.	I am the flow.

Who Are These Authors?

Rev. Dr. Paul Hasselbeck currently serves as the Dean, Spiritual Education and Enrichment, at Unity Village, MO. He helped found the only English-speaking Unity Church in Puerto Rico. Dr. Hasselbeck is the author of *Point of Power: Practical Metaphysics to Help You Transform Your Life and Realize Your Magnificence,* which is published in English and Spanish, and has also edited and amplified *Metaphysics I* and *Metaphysics II,* the textbooks used to teach Metaphysics at Unity Village. In his free time, Paul enjoys working out, surfing eBay, collecting vintage art pottery, and enjoying a huge flock of exotic birds. He lives in Kansas City with his partner, Martin.

Bil Holton, Ph.D., currently shares spiritual leadership responsibilities with his wife, Cher, in the growing Unity Spiritual Life Center in Durham, NC. As a student of metaphysics for over 30 years, Dr. Holton is the author of many books, including *Metaphysical Versions* of all four Gospels. On a personal note, Bil enjoys ballroom dancing, golfing, and taking "Indiana Jones vacations" such as white water rafting, sky diving, and fire-walking. Bil and Cher live in Durham, NC, and enjoys visits with their two sons, loving daughters-in-law, and two incredible grandchildren!

You can learn more about Bil by visiting his website: www.metaphysicalbible.net.

Index

GET OVER IT!